ECHOES IN A SUNLIT GORGE

Other Books by Denham Grierson
published by Coventry Press

Turning in Time
Sharing Water by the River
Music From a Breaking Wave
Chronicles of Light & Air
Star Fall in a Midnight Sky

POEMS OF MEETING

ECHOES IN A SUNLIT GORGE

DENHAM GRIERSON

COVENTRY
PRESS

Published in Australia by
Coventry Press
33 Scoresby Road
Bayswater VIC 3153

ISBN 9781922589507

Copyright © Denham Grierson 2024

All rights reserved. Other than for the purposes and subject to the conditions prescribed under the *Copyright Act*, no part of this publication may be reproduced, stored in a retrieval system, or transmitted in any form or by any means, electronic, mechanical, photocopying, recording or otherwise, without the prior permission of the publisher.

Catalogue-in-Publication entry is available from the National Library of Australia
http://catalogue.nla.gov.au

Cover design by Ian James – www.jgd.com.au
Text design by Coventry Press
Set in Tex Gyre Pagella

Printed in Australia

Contents

Foreword	11
Acknowledgments	13
Introduction	14
DAWN	17
Gorge	18
Night Time	19
Rock Art	20
Ghost Gum	22
Ghost Train	23
Anomy	24
Foreverness	26
Longing	28
Space	30
Earthquake	31
New Years Day	32
Flock	34
Letting Go	36
Wind Gust	37
Crown	38

Migrants	39
New World	40
Protector	42
Pandemic	43
Kiss	44
Trust	46
Anatomy of Wanting	47
Wish	48
Second World War Memories	49
Reflections on Ecclesiastes 3	50
Judgment	52
Planted	53
Away	54
Music to our ears	55
Mystery	56
Lighted Abyss	57
Coming	58
Awake	60
Travelling	61

NOON — 63

Time for Leaving	64
Something to be Heard	65
Habitat	66
Disease	67
Understanding	68

Listening	70
Marrow	71
Beginning Again	72
Creek	73
Imagine	74
Safe	76
Futures	78
Tomorrow's Promise	80
Away	81
Flow	82
Signifier	83
One	84
Fall	85
Another Place	86
Cave	87
Suffering	88
Other	89
Carers on Night Duty	90
Beauty Salon	91
Day of Rest	92
Pageantry	94
Memory Loss	95
Simplicity	96
Next	97
Trajectory	98
End Time	99

SUNSET 101

If Tomorrow Never Comes	102
Contemplating	103
Unknowing	104
As Is	105
Only a Wind	106
Enigma	107
Grammar	108
Old Friends	109
Pick and Shovel Destiny	110
Music	111
Shipwrecked	112
Birthday Party	114
Dictator	115
Whistle Blower	116
Brawl	117
Paying Attention	118
Growling Grass Frog Enigma	119
Suddenly	120
Attention	121
Time Passing	122
Sanctuary	123
Trial	124
Dream	126
Jazz Piano	127

Daffodil Season	128
Mary	129
Doll's House	130
Remembrance	132
Slaughter	133
Cathedral	134
Ent	135
Stories	136

Foreword

My first encounter with Denham was about forty years ago at the United Faculty of Theology, Ormond College, Melbourne University, where he taught me about religious education. In the Common Room, he encouraged my interest in poetry by saying something like, 'Start with an image and find the words to explore it'.

> *Poetry is to theology*
> *as rain is to cloud,*
> *a foundational essence*
> (Protector)

We have kept up with his thinking over the years through his numerous publications. One might expect a slowing down of creativity in later life. Not so with Denham. Now poetry has become one of his passions! His poetry output has intensified to a marvellous extent. I'm delighted in recent years that we have been able to share poetry at the monthly meeting of the Bloomin' Bards, a group of exploring poets that meet in homes and cafes.

This volume attests that the welling up from the depths of experience, acute observation and emotional richness continues apace. The range of subjects explored would be surprising to some, but not if you've come to know Denham through his previous writing.

The poems have a discipline of form that is his own. We find many starting points in his words, each reflecting an experience, always seeking the meaning below the surface. In the breadth of his fascination, he explores the dimensions of time, family, love and loss, belonging, despair, hope, disillusionment, joy, longing, and healing – among other subjects. Some are analytical, some deeply personal, all make connections.

When you read this volume, you will appreciate the full range, the broad church of mind. It is not possible to read this volume quickly. Each poem needs to be savoured; like medication, take one or two in the morning, and/or at bedtime.

Savour, enjoy, be surprised, challenged, enlightened. Accept his invitation to become his companion in travelling.

We find ourselves in a far country divided
A wilderness of spirit bereft of direction ...

Let us become a new people setting out
Travelling through time and space toward a destiny
Unafraid of risk or suffering, seeking a growing place
Which will gather all into its welcoming inclusiveness.
                                            (Travelling)

I'd like to end up in the same place as Denham.

Peter Sanders

Peter Sanders is a poet, scientist, intellectual explorer; and an Ordained Minister of the Uniting Church in Australia.

Acknowledgments

Coventry Press, for once again supporting another volume of poems in a difficult commercial time.

Once again also, the editor of these volumes of poems, Hugh McGinlay, who, like old wine, only gets better. Peter Sanders, poet, scientist, explorer, and Uniting Church Minister, who willingly and effortlessly wrote the Foreword with insight and clarity. To my travelling poetic companions, Andy Tiver and John Cranmer, always vigilant, always searching, always supportive. To my wife Mavis, and my daughter Susan, who contribute in their several ways to this production of many voices.

To all of the above, and to a wider circle of friends and encouragers, who make the process of envisioning a new day, a new world, a living hope, I extend my heartfelt thanks. All of us are smarter than one of us.

Introduction

In his work, *Opus Posthumus*, the American author and poet Wallace Stevens advances three propositions.

1. The world about us would be desolate except for the world within us.
2. The major poetic idea in the world is, and always has been, the idea of God.
3. After one has abandoned a belief in God, poetry is the essence which takes its place as life's redemption.

Apart from the disjuncture between proposition 2 and 3, a process of mistaking the cart for the horse, Stevens is advancing the audacious claim that poetry is that which will ultimately save us.

By the exercise of creative imagination, we make contact with an epiphanic dimension within that grants us purpose.

That dimension, accessible through poetry, leads us to a recognition of multiple purposes in life beyond the merely utilitarian, leading to a fulfilment or our expressive potential, a compelling beyond-ness revealing itself in all that we can imagine.*

---

* Many of the ideas in this Introduction, and some in following poems, have their source in Charles Taylor's classic text, *Sources of the Self*, Cambridge University Press.1989. With grateful acknowledgment.

This viewpoint rests on proposition 1 above, which in its turn paraphrases a line of Rilke in his seventh poem in the *Duino Elegies*: *'Nowhere, beloved, will world be but within us'*. The idea of poetry's quest then is laid out against a contemporary world view that gives credence only to instrumental attainment in a neutral environment which can be manipulated to serves our purposes. The outcome is a loss of intentionality reducing culture to a shallowness of what we choose to communicate. We fail to see that the self-fulfilment mantras of the me generation lead only to emptiness and what has been called 'a destroying self inflicted wound'. We suffocate the spirit within us.

What poetry reaches for is a deeply personal human habitat in a world that addresses and seizes us. The power of creative imagination is the power to transform ordinary experience by the creation of a unique, intuitive language which carries a vision of depth and purpose. To facilitate an unveiling. To make the hidden known. Traditionally we have used the symbol God to give expression to this mysterious ground of all we know and intend, *'a sense of sublime/ of something far more deeply fused'*, to quote Wordsworth.

It is this resonance that seeks to capture our attention embedded in the lived experience of daily life. A profound telling of depth in the nature of things, and in ourselves. *'Inward goes the way of mystery.'* Poetry is one of those sources that enfold us with a sense of surrounding grace found in the compass of ordinary experience. The poems in this volume seek to call us to this presentness, inviting a quiet listening, a ready stillness toward that which is beyond and within, a grateful attendance at the banquet set before us. It happens in its own genre of expression, and contains what is still true – that the greatest message is not just about the idea of God but the presence of God in whatever language that carries this virtue.

It was W. B. Yeats who raised the question explored in the text of these poems. 'How can we know the dancer from the dance?' Perhaps more compelling – 'How can we join the dance to find the wholeness that it offers?'

DAWN

GORGE

The Gorge, more ancient than can be told
Basks in a bright sun stretching its meandering length
Remembering thousands upon thousands of silent years
Resting in the Gorge's outstretched hands, trustingly
Remembering also the coming of bird flocks
Holding onto scoured, warm, red-ochre sides
Land animals chattering incomprehensibly at calm pools
Dark night creatures lapping up their crystal life

Humming in prehended consciousness
Songs now imprinted in his grainy flesh
Hearing the harmony of Mother Earth
Singing corroboree upon a cosmic stage
Addressing stars well planted in garden skies
Telling stories of long ago and once upon a time
Sharing a welcoming in a sun browned skin

NIGHT TIME

In the darkness the stars are agitating
The night sky with their boisterousness again
Leaping, sliding, falling, blinking, flashing, hiding
Shouting to us a message difficult to interpret
With its venerable accent of wonder

Who thought of this extravaganza
And just like this, and no other
If you embrace it now, tomorrow it will be different
Novelty and creation have little time for repetition
Habits, rituals, eternal truths, immovable conclusions

The splendour captured not by flat explanation
But by the ingenuity of artistic imagination
Making and re-making its boundlessness
Diving into inexhaustible depths
To bring to the surface a pearl of great price

ROCK ART

Art, sign of civilisation
Second creation on rock and stone
Birth of the mind's expansion
Representing blood and bone

Securing place, securing time
Reaching for a world becoming
Spreading out encoded patterns
Making real perceptual seeming

Ochre mouth-sprayed on a wall
Icons painted by frayed sticks
Hidden in the mists of aeons
Life rising up beyond life's risk

Shaman bodied, sacred calling
To capture spirit in cave lime
Spirit womb of human beings
Life painting life sublime

Abundant flow, creative image
Shaped into a human face
Presence speaking out of darkness
Light transforming inert space

Transcendence in the slender line
A scratch upon eternity
Explosion of awakening thought

Trembling touch of certainty

Ritual dancing, social tracing
Promise of a coming time
Pointing to the heart of mystery
Proclaiming vision of the blind

Here the poetry of our kind
Beauty in its primal form
Holding treasures of the soul
Evaporating in a mobile storm

GHOST GUM

We knew they had souls once
Distinct personalities and personal stories
The Ghost Gum rose high into the sky
White-skinned, smooth, dancing, welcoming
As female as glass slippers, leaving me
Embarrassed I did not know her name

Tho' each time I passed
She greeted me as a friend, shaping
Patterned light upon the path, guiding my feet
(As had her forebears in distant landscapes)
To water, and yellow tailed cockatoos
Who knew her family scattered wide

Across red ochre plains in far country
Protecting the fragile earth
The soft wondering of emergent life
As always, I stopped to pay homage
As always, leaving embarrassed I did not know
Her name

GHOST TRAIN

The hungry mouth of the Ghost ride tunnel
Open, dark, foreboding, waits our presence
Terror and dread on one hand
Excitement and anticipation on the other
We contemplate the numinous ambiguity
Offering life and death, confinement or freedom

To lose one's self or find another
To secure a steadfast truth, or possess illusion
To confront power insecure, pleasure that never satisfies
Tempted by elusive ecstasy, deceitful bliss
Lured beyond a proper rhythm of organic processes
Haunted by phantoms, emotional, rationalistic, coldly ambitious

Offering numbing materialism, escape from necessity and death
A special status, a special fate, a special entitlement
Billowing steam obscuring the waiting furies
Illusory, without substance, form or light
Denizens of the dark who await, unaware
There is a word that slays them all

ANOMY

In the slow swing of summer heat
When the air seems just off the boil
Flowers wilt under the sun, leaves curling
There is suspension of toil

A heaviness falls upon the earth
As if a bell rings closing time
Birds eschew flight, insects do not sing
There is no pattern, rhythm, or rhyme

Across dry paddocks a heat wave simmering
Crackling in the windless breeches
The dam is shrinking, afraid to draw attention
Stern absence of purpose. Who knows what it teaches

A suffocating waiting that takes the breath away
No desire to act, to move, to stir
Nature appears to give up on intentions
To glance indifferently off buckling branches bare

Listless in the spreading shade
Denied the will to save the passing hour
Captive of an impasse in a weather fugue
A pause to wonder. What if the world turned sour

Empty, hollow, afflicted by thirst
Felled by heat-sucking energy
The burden of breathing in a trance

Is there in this blockage synergy

Nothing to report. Nothing to say
Dust fills the air, effort has gone astray
Inertia fills the blasted day
When will the wheels turn, life come out to play

I cannot lift my spirit to reply
Time passes without note or soft impress
Perhaps anomy of a natural kind
To school us to stillness and to rest

FOREVERNESS

It is the same misunderstanding repeated
With righteous conviction and ignoble exclusion
This is our land, not to be surrendered
By Voice or Treaty, by law, or malfeasance
Unaware that no one owns the land
It is itself the sovereignty we claim

There should only be one flag, he avows
Meaning the one of colonial possession
The Southern Cross turned over in defeat
Unwilling to recognise a compelling symbol
Of a people one with the land they tread
Blood red, yellow alight, black essence

The cry of 'mine' blind to the judgment
Of thousands of years, lives lived in harmony
With Mother Earth, bound by the heart's sharing
Consecrated by generations of giving care
Who understood the Dreaming call
The deep soul-song in the dawn's awakening

Only dance can tell, only silence confer
The limitless surrender, the unfolding love
Only the story, mythic in shape and form
Can carry the water of its life
The fire of its heart
The compulsion of its sacredness

If we enter humbly perhaps we can grasp
The timeless claim of repeated seasons
To venerate majestic otherness
Carved into rock, dotted in swirled patterns
Rainbow Snake, creative presence, coiled
Holding all that is, and has been, and will be

Our land, our flag, our history a claim
Of blind ignorance, festering in entitlement
Convinced possession, gained by bait and gun
Justification spilled from a shrunken soul
A stone heart that does not understand
We have no permanence. Only the land has that

LONGING

We are unable to comprehend today's world
And no one has the courage
To delineate the future, not having words

Looking back is little help
For fog obscures the vision
Of those who went before

We have lost focus
Assaulted as we are
By jumbled complexity

That has no thread
No wind-vane pointing
For the world has fallen away

Bear with me for a moment
I am not saying that love and goodness
Are in short supply

Only that we are compromised
By pre-nuptials and cynical divorce
Driven by avarice and advantage

That which by its nature, permanent
Rendered impermanent
Devastated by diminishment

You can trust Winter's end
And Spring's youthful venturing
But not human fidelity

Still, the daffodils bloom again
And gathered, can be given
In love's gesture, with joy

Here in this simple moment
Proof of the deepest longing
We may yet find again

SPACE

We need to make room for space
Or, more correctly, gather it
In order to give it to others

A time of planting soul-habitation
Which only love can nourish
A space, needy, thread-bare, and silent

A task of restoring radiance
That brings the world back to life
And asks, 'where are you placing yourself'

Sleeping in the blackberry patch
Or on the edge of the raft
Looking outward, trustingly

We are in a time of dark forbidding
Determined to kill the inwardness of things
Needing the space that reaches out to us

EARTHQUAKE

The earthquake is an act of God
They say, a declared judgment
Ignoring the shoddy workmanship
Of collapsed buildings
The disregard of regulations
Money passed to officials
Paid to avoid compliance
Ignoring warnings from experts
Disregarding the regions risks
For the sake of profits
An act of God?
A plague on all their houses

NEW YEARS DAY

On new years day
The fires got away
The fires burn
And twist and turn

Black heaven's scowl
Unleashed burning howl
A terrifying sound
Across the fire ground
The fires burn
And twist and turn

A Government promise
The coal man cometh
We act with purpose
And retain a surplus
The fires burn
And twist and turn

Treetops in flame
None to blame
No more climate change
Than wombat mange
The fires burn
And twist and turn

Fulfilment of prophesy

Dismissed as fantasy
Firestorms run amok
Flipping a fire truck
The fires burn
And twist and turn

Grass fires flow unchecked
Destroying homes, destroying flocks
Infrastructure's blackened scars
Multiple roads blocked with cars
The fires burn
And twist and turn

Sea evacuation
Firies exhaustion
A people bond together
Victims of malevolent weather
The fires burn
And twist and turn

When all the fires are done
We have just begun
Nightmares of destruction
Memories of devastation
Of when the fires burned
And twisted and turned

FLOCK

The thousand strong flock of corellas
Conquer the Park lawns
With one cacophonous descent

Occupying trees, bushes, bridges
With a cocky exuberance
Not far short of Kingly arrogance

By some morphic resonance
They lower heads as one
Feasting on green provenance

Always the harsh, coarse chorus rumbling
Undercurrent of all restless play
Leaving no doubt of sovereignty

A common will holding them united
Whose source defies intelligence
A knowing congress, a flighted coterie

Then as one, they rise commanded
Shouting raucously a fresh intent
Circling in formation, suddenly hell bent

A heavy weight lifts from twilight shoulders
Space expanding, breathing again
Restoring tranquil silence descends

I sit at the edge of the Wetland
Considering a vast company as one
Reflecting on my own species, divided, broken, undone

LETTING GO

These days I am dropping things a lot
Or is it letting them go
Because they escape focus
Or because they no longer matter
Is it a case of losing meaning
Or a profound disinterest
Because they do not address the centre
Have no compulsion that we must hold tightly
What seems irrelevant when
Our relationship to them has died
Is it they are slipping into a past
No longer evocative, no longer alive

Before a new birth into what is free
For which, as yet, I have no name

WIND GUST

Wind gusts tutor the autumn leaves
Gathering them into coloured bunches
Unified by tumbling heaves
Spirit-bonded temporary sculptures

As if a sentient consciousness
Dwells within this bee-hive heap
Rolling as an entity of togetherness
Wholeness in a riotous leap

Seemingly, awareness of direction
A guiding purpose, vital destiny
Dancing along narrow sections
Of woodland paths, balletically

Suddenly the wind departs, the spirit flees
Leaves atomise into disharmony
Communal centredness collapses by degrees
Only an illusion of intentionality

The atoms that constitute our being-ness
Carry a heritage of millions of years
Already they signal my fading humanness
As I enter into the travelling winds career

CROWN

There are parallel universes
To our own
Playing out countless reverses

So an ancient formation
The mystic crown
A parallel creation

MIGRANTS

Each year they travel thousands of miles
From Russia tho' these last years
Fewer numbers arrive to dwell
In habitats along Australian beaches

These places become hazardous for nesting
With human commerce and rampaging dogs
Despising their space, troubling their calm
A repeat of stations on the way

Across arduous stretches forests are gone
Resting trees destroyed, real estate advances
Fires, toxic spraying, climate unrest
Inevitably the flock declines

Driven by genetic surging to make the trip
To warmer climes, there to raise their young
And now, a desperate struggle, a friendless passage
Beset with snares, poisons, and desolation

Still the flock falls from the sky
Upon familiar landscapes, safely alive
Fossick, dabble in the sun, lay their eggs
Warm in the sun. Half their usual number this time

NEW WORLD

Without warning I am living in a world
I do not recognise. Was not prepared for. Or expected

Overnight the world I knew vanished
Fell over under the weight of the digital

Strangely, I live in the world I love
While now the virtual world commands my senses

My world has changed into something else
I have to learn new rules to pay my bills

As if I have been sent a message that reads, come
Without instructions on how to get there

This new world has its logic that escapes the old
Making my logic more and more illogical

Does the world I know still exist
Is it taken seriously as something worthy

I am like a bird in a time cage set free
Seeking to inhabit unfamiliar terrain

There to survive amid confusion
There to learn new realities nearing the incomprehensible

When did they change the rules, lift the curtain
On a new story, a new plot, prescribe new perceptions

Who pulled the lever, re-routing the train
Without us noticing the death of civility

The rise of entitlement, the disappearance of community
Or fearfully, no stated destination

PROTECTOR

Poetry is to theology
As rain is to cloud
A foundational essence
Capable of multiple forms
Sleet, hail, drizzle, snow
That cannot be pressed
Into solid, immobile, architecture

Bestowing life by elusive conversation
Giving to the declaration of meaning
A constant mandate to
Interpret afresh the vitality
Of old and new
Bearing the task unending
Within our blood flow, our mobile bones

What to keep
What to throw away

PANDEMIC

Jessup came to the hospital
When I was safe once more
The plague, he said, is widespread
A world of RATS and closed doors

I told him of my headaches
Shortness of breath and aches
Immunity is health, he said
Wear a mask for all our sakes

Remember in your weakness
How good it was before
We gave little thought to the virus
Which prowls from shore to shore

How thin the line between
This estate and the other
Disaster by all reckoning
We saw no cause to bother

KISS

It is inescapable. We are nothing but air
Space cavorting in each atom. Our wholeness
Never really there, a phantom concreteness

All of our structures and connections
Are tissue thin, a flow of energy
Itself falling away, a disappearing lightness

We do not entertain our vulnerabilities
With any seriousness. Stripped bare
To our essence is no destination

Why do we honour matter so royally
Physicality our major preoccupation
As if the one place we can call home

A deteriorating asset that entered into
At its deepest is only vista, distant view
An energetic openness, a wideness of sky

Holding somehow a boundless complexity
Of feeling affect and reaching desire
Compelled by intentionality

Are we those without secured reality
Presence solid as a mistral fade
Capable of compelling integrity

Tap the taut drum, skin stretched
Over nothingness, follow the sound
Into an eternal cadence

And ask: am I a nothingness
Discerned by sound only
In an illusory selfhood

Crying into a founding abyss
Called into a mysterious being-ness
By the gentleness of a loving kiss

TRUST

There is in the room
A full emptiness
Carrying a trace of eucalyptus
An emptiness offering nothing else

There are no comings or goings
A nothingness coloured with memory
A nothingness that is not nothing

Here is the fullness of life
Filled with presence
That leaves no calling card

I am as full of this emptiness
As the sky is of air
An absence I give my life to

ANATOMY OF WANTING

It is the want of it that guides our journey
Not the possession for that we never have
Hunger for food survives all meals
Thirst for drink continues ever after

More properly, a hint of what we seek
A tantalising glimpse, a beckoning promise
Perfume trace upon the air, an echo
From a hidden mystery swells

Like the siren call of far off horns
A longing for an other-ness unknown
The sweet taste of possibility, an imagined meeting
All but reflections of an infinite beyond

From the secret vault of lonely hearts
A touch of fantasy, as real as any real
A reach for what inspires, a grasp for our desires
All in this dying flesh, its very blood

A summons from that realm, never embodied
A song of ethereal beauty never sung
A signature deep within all stories told
A rhythm of eternity, an unknown tongue

In our emptiness this is our possession
An answering love for what first came to us
We cannot hope to name what is ineffable
Only travel to the welcome that we trust

WISH

Chinese whispers are sprouting
Within the gathered news
Chinese whispers are shouting
In homesteads and castles and mews

Russian shells are exploding
Bringing death to the towns
Russian shells are destroying
With the aim to bring everything down

North Korean flags are flying
In villages poor and dismayed
Sky rockets rising, flaring
To destroy those declared Satan raised

Source of our deepest concerning
Whispers, shells and public display
Descend into dreams scarcely moving
Wishing them to go away

Is there hope in our asking
Is there a restoring way
Is there a new day dawning
That heralds a peace-loving day

SECOND WORLD WAR MEMORIES

In the streets of our town on ANZAC day
Every house was mourning
They gathered in solemn groups for worship as
Dawn broke into mourning
We did not understand PTS
The slow march of deep distress
By ten o'clock most would be drunk
Searching for redemption beneath the funk
Of survivor guilt before it carried them away
Remorse and hate of Huns, Ities and Japs
Yet somehow recognising them as victims also, perhaps
All crushed by the horror of war
No medalled glory delivered as promised before
Only pain and grief and loss
Depression, suicide and worse
They hugged and embraced each other
In the bathroom my mother cried for her brother
This in the deprivation and suffering we endured
Despair that the curse of war ensured
The bugle note, alone pure, carried regret
And as a child, futility I could not forget
Courage, sacrifice, to secure our future
But in the streets of our town, on ANZAC day
Only anguish and memories of slaughter

REFLECTIONS ON ECCLESIASTES 3

Is it true that everything
Is suitable for its time
When that which is
Already has been
That which is to be
Already is

So in time, the time we inhabit
We live timelessly
Repeating patterns as if new
Hoping for those things
We already have
Trying to find all things
Suitable, amidst everything
That has its allotted time
And seems eternally elusive

In this timeliness
Of suitability
God passes, seeking
What has gone before
To that still point
Which is to be and
Already is

Past and future
In our minds

Nothing to be added
Nothing taken away
Everything underlining
It is suitable
For its time

The dying that we
Might live
The gathering of stones
In a time of throwing away
Here is the riddle of suitability
Suitable for what
To time's servitude?

Or is it possible
A gift not understood
Time is given to us
That which we call now
For everything this is its season

JUDGMENT

Rich hay bales
Lie negligently in the sun
In somewhat lines
Upon the denuded carpet of the grass

An insouciance of the complete
The full, the contented, basking
In their value and significance
Spread open to their mother's milk

Chatting across openness
Conscious of their noted presence
The completion of summer harvest
Summa cum laude conferred

Tomorrow loaded upon trucks
Bodies, hurled down, split open
Large herds will consume their totality
Drought's other judgment

PLANTED

'Poetry evokes out of words the resonance of the primordial word.'

Gerhard Hauptmann

The soil gives life to the flower
But the plant pays it no mind
The child nourished in the womb's bower
Has no interest in what holds or binds

The musician creates a new song
By means of chords taken for granted
We are living, travelling along
Not noticing resources pre-planted

Surrounded by love's generosity
Caring for, fueling our flight
My life is a protected propensity
Sustained by Nature's delight

Let me turn then, in repentance of insight
To acknowledge these forces that gift me my life
Caring for those others condemned to the twilight
For want of a loving goodnight

AWAY

I want to run away
To escape
From the weight of expectations

To sit without agendas
Or the need to justify
Idleness

To feel free of responsibilities
And duties
Not to worry or fuss
Or fear

But it is futile
Wherever I turn
I carry myself with me

MUSIC TO OUR EARS

There are parts of the self slipping away
Memory now fickle, sometimes petulant
Sometimes fading into nothingness
Names as elusive as bush rats
Exhaustion at encounters with the web
Despair at the lack of recall of
Significant dates and strategic anniversaries

It is a matter of inner absence
Tasks half done, promises neglected
Birthday cards unsent, grave sites not visited
The historical narrative, holed as old socks
In the gaps a misty recall of pretend
As much the son of fantasy as the daughter of facts
Seeking to build security upon shifting sand

There is nothing more restoring than the bells
Always the same story that they tell

MYSTERY

Mystery is only that which we do not know
Given time we will penetrate its obscurity
Explain its complexity and know it completely

A point of view misunderstanding the word
For by definition mystery is that defying explanation
Not just the unknown but an active address
That seizes us compulsively, defying all translation

Stretch out your arm. How you did that
Is susceptible to explanation by multiple avenues
None of which unveil how you did what you did

A you that escapes discovery
As elusive as moonlight on the forest
Or sunlight on a breaking wave
Or loving one another for no obvious reason

Reaching back to the principle of life
Spirit that moves the sphere of the heart
The given-ness that leads us, child like, into mystery

LIGHTED ABYSS

Franz Kafka referred to the Christ event
As a lighted abyss
From which we must avert our eyes
Lest we fall into it

Not recognising that the lighted abyss
Falls into us, compellingly
Light possessing every fibre and molecule
Bringing to birth a consciousness of self

As a candle burns its own substance
So our flesh dies in giving forth light
Learning in the radiance of its possession
We are loved

COMING

New spaces are being prepared for tomorrow
In which we might find ourselves challenged anew
Not on the vellum plan of yesterday
The barbed wire entanglement of an empty today
But shaped around that central burning focus, for which
We have used historically, the symbol God

The superstructure has vanished
The very core of certainty disintegrated
Despite belief. Only provisional anyway

We built on rock, as advised
Only to feel it crumble into sand
Beneath our feet, threatening a worm hole
Into a chasm we knew was there
But would not believe was efficacious

Indeed the centre cannot hold
The foundations shake, as wind swept grass
But what holds all together is not disturbed
Beyond our need to shape and plane, to
Bind and cut reality. We hold only illusion
A distorted image of what truly abides
In a guise, a coming we cannot name
In a form elusive we call incarnation

Change in its formlessness is water blessed

Liquid in its flowing, sea-tide in its restlessness
In order that we might lift our heads
From trivial pursuits to greet the boundlessness
Of novelty's expansion, calling us to come
Before that which transforms is nailed into place again

AWAKE

Rise to morning's new beginning
Creation's welcome come to play
Open to its free giving
Offering another day

Here the celebration starting
Foretaste of the choir's display
See the flight, the wings of gladness
Eagle, osprey, bright blue jay

Honour the pattern of life's forming
Spirit renewing time's array
Following footsteps onward leading
Christ child joining our affray

Feel the inward life bestowing
Energy to make your way
Hearing in your heart's beating
Tasks and aims that must not stray

Listen to the trumpets playing
Calling you to your assay
Church bells chiming, far horn calling
Grow and act and dance and pray

So we rise in concert singing
Children made much more than clay
Called into God's intention
In all we do and share and say

TRAVELLING

We find ourselves in a far country divided
A wilderness of spirit bereft direction
We need path finders, explorers
Who lead us to fresh springs of thought

Away from tawdry expectations, deceitful illusions
We do not need more gadgets to prevail
Memory of a lost home far richer than hollow entertainment
Reminding us of shared caring, an intimate conclave

Let us become a new people setting out
Travelling through time and space toward a destiny
Unafraid of risk and suffering, seeking a growing place
Which will gather all into its welcoming inclusiveness

NOON

TIME FOR LEAVING

It is time for leaving
We must go today
Heath flowering
Sign of beginning

We are not ready
Bewildered by choice
Possessions to be shed
You cannot take much

Step into tomorrow's day
A waiting buried treasure
Gift from past travellers
Handing us a living future

Sacrifices must be made
Inclusion sought, hospitality shared
Humility fostered, in this strange realm
Where all will be taken, all given again

SOMETHING TO BE HEARD

If there is hearing, there is something to be heard
If there is looking, something to look upon
The leaping of the gazelle, the gliding of the swan

If there is caring, someone to receive care
Loving for the loveless, sharing for the herd
Food waiting for the hungry, bird seed for the birds

Hope in the waving of the drowning self
If healing there is wholeness
Comfort in our sorrow, angel on the shelf

If there is seeking, the desired to be found
Or knocking a door to open wide
Timber of the oak tree, key to the great inside

The thirst of constant lack, that which meets its need
In every blood flow a living heart
And in each conceiving, one unique who stands apart

There is in every dissonance a balance that can save
And in every wandering a pathway to the inn
In the chorus of all things a song that always sings

HABITAT

The slam of the hammer tells
Of workmen creating habitat
Overhead the kite swings
Silent, responding to habitat
Roses, bursting red, being habitat
We, in our turn, ingesting habitat

Sound, silence, spell of space
Enclosing us in belonging
A coat of many colours
Vortex of manifold dimensions
Boundless in extent and hospitality
Including us in

DISEASE

It is the text of the disease
I am trying to interpret
An inter-action seeking understanding
Of its invasion focused on killing, only killing
A descent without purpose or warning
Leaving us devastated by its incremental violence
Casting upon our every breath, a voiceless sadness

Can we have a relationship with such a soul-less hunger
A transaction that unearths some shred of meaning
Rather than icy possession without life
Where no covenant is possible, no warming touch
Or celebration of mutuality. Here is only
Pain and loss and ending
No healing calm or redemptive pause

A time of quick hail, slow fire
An inwardness with no song or lyre

UNDERSTANDING

The only way to understand
Is to stand ready
To participate from the inside
For when everything is outside
Nothing is truly knowable

We were meant to go deep in
As the way to uncover signs
To interpret what is happening
We were given to ourselves
As something to construct

To develop a self image
Seeking to understand
What sort of being we are
A power to interpret
Midwife of aliveness

This constant struggle to know
Is a journey of discovery
Of our self and our world
Decisively, our place in it
As a meaning centre

A wrestle with potentiality
A striving to name freedom
As a way of understanding

Who it is we are
And what we might become

So, standing under
In order to understand
Tuning in to our own broadcasts
To discern what might emerge
In a world that is our life space

Experiencing the vivid moment
That carries the hidden-ness
Of our becoming whole
Growing into the vitality we call identity
That inwardness that understands

LISTENING

The soft rain burbling outside
Trying to communicate
With my sleeplessness
A visitation of night speak

Insomnia has its own debate
Wrapped in existence's warm cloak
Having dialogue with otherness
Not hearing, even if the rain spoke

Yet the inner and outer are one
A mutuality of meeting
Entering into the mystery of existing things
And wondering again, Who is listening

MARROW

I never did prayer well
Except for the gnawing of its bone
More effort than nourishment
Which came more surely by calm ponds
In twilight, recognising that mystery
Remains mysterious, no matter how earnestly
I seek the marrow of its life
Finding instead that the fat, plump honey
Of the hive gave more nourishment
Because it came out of shared intimacy
A sweet gathering from all over the wet-lands
Telling me that in matters
Of the divine, sought so fervently
Chronicle intimacies are at hand

BEGINNING AGAIN

We see the world as we are
Not as it is, for it is infinitely changing
We cannot hold its complexity secure
Within our limited awareness

A conceit of language and tone prevails
Seeking depth and ground with persistence
In a daily gestation, unable to find conclusions
To be reassured our vessel is not empty

I conclude I am beginning each day again
Learning as a beginner, having an intuition
Of the young, that open reception, transcending logic
Entering in like a child who plays with abandon,
trustingly

CREEK

Jessup stopped the car at the creek's edge
The bridge swept away. Surging brown water
Gushing across the damaged road

They cut down the old growth trees
In the high country, flood waters stripping
The soil without vegetation or undergrowth
To hold back destruction of the landscape

It was the women who took action
Finding out which councillors changed
Their votes against established policy
Who took gifts or shares
Those granted special favours

We looked down the creek's traverse
Banks cut away, savaged, silt and
Rubbish mounting in choked pockets
No wonder we have a species sunset clause
Said Jessup

IMAGINE

Imagine God as energy
Pulsing, electric, thrusting quickness
Vitality of the smallest atom's torque and stress
Quanta of cosmic expansion, wind, light, warmth
Inner effervescence of spirit-ness, impetuously acting
That nurtures our quickened consciousness alive

Conceive of God as power
Stupendous potency, force, vigour
Efficacious in jab, wallop, smack, and push
Soft radiance to a questioning child
Cogency to a questing mind, swift lightning flash
Holding dominion in a welcoming open palm

Explore God as light
Illumination, flicker, epiphany, incandescence
Compellingly resplendent, glimmer, sparkle, twinkle
Lustre of our seeing, shine of our hope
Sun-burst extravaganza, water's glare, darkness glow
Luminous centre of our knowing, flame, flare

Reflect on God as future
Not yet to be, eternal promise, timelessness
Near to hand, constant rhythm of tomorrow
Calling, compelling, seizing, waiting
Potentiality, insistent, undisclosed
Which hungering demands attention

Gather within God as life
Wholeness, foreverness, incarnation
Flight, reach, wonder, assurance within our bones
Heart beat, blood flow, awareness, extant
Deep within, beyond, perpetually there
Symphony of our being, song of our love

SAFE

I have no words for safe
Or being safe or safer
That sense of inner peace
Deep trust of the world's intent
Despite unnamed threats surrounding
The perimeter of consciousness

Emerging out of feral depths
When sleep disarms us
In the defenceless small hours
Doubt arises, unchecked within
Not banished by love's assurance
Fantastic and surreal forces grim

Deep anxiety excited
Well understands our frailty
Helpless before marching foes
Marshalling in martial rows
Conquering a city protected only
By that carapace called love

Here is the hush of reassurance
Warm arms, sweet words, a being-for
Bringing light into dark places
Overthrowing the feared shuddering
Filled with nameless movings
That only love can overcome

Out of the clear blue sky, a strike
In the deceitful eyes, the shark fin flash
Sustenance withdrawn without announcement
The foundations of our confidence crash
And we are undone by terror
If we do not know sanctuary

We receive the promise of protection
Against enemies at the gate
Here the constancy of will stands
In danger for our sake
A love as constant as the day is long
Woven strands that tell us we belong

FUTURES

We live in the epoch of the end
Of business as usual
The axe severs before and after
Continuity of the then and now
No longer tradition honoured, expected, or allowed

The assured course of events
Subsides beneath a merciless brown flood
Carrying treacherous, destroying mud
That suffocates and eliminates dreams
Futures are white boards wiped clean

Gone what we were before, with ambitions and hopes
We are no longer traders of trusty reputations
We must re-define expectations, plans, intentions
Unsure of who we are, defenceless, stripped bare, lost
No longer feeling safe, no longer certain of tomorrow

Brought to our knees by epidemic, endemic corruption
Fire and flood and economic ruin
Innocent people destroyed by purposeless wars
A time of havoc, disaster, destruction
There is no matter of factness, only abandonment

In this cataclysm what can be trusted
Where can we place our feet, where find assurance
We are no longer what we were

We cannot cast a future viable for ourselves
We rise into a morning of anomy

In this whirlpool of disintegrated expectation
There are promises long distrusted
What is lost can unexpectedly be found
What is sought, miraculously discovered
What is assured, life given for tomorrow

TOMORROW'S PROMISE

It is at noon
That the light and the dark
Are balanced
No shadow falls
To alert us to our
True situation

High noon when heroism
Must fight unaided that
Which seeks to destroy possibility

The attainment of equilibrium
Denies us knowledge
Surely only suffering
Or the fear of God
Plant the seed of love
Which gestates in the shadow

Birthing in the light
Stooping down despite the pain
To pluck the full blossom
Of our life's gift

It is evening without redemption
Darkness covers the earth
It is dawn, the third day
Promise of tomorrows flowering

AWAY

Today she was not there
Abstracted, absent
Occupying a clouded distance
That has no visitors pass
No welcome mat, no brass knocker
The disease keeping the door locked

I felt as if I was a bottle
Full of love to share, things to say
Knocked over, contents running slowly out
Onto parched land, disappearing forever
The diminishing of my life with her own
The last thing she would want or desire

FLOW

I do not want to be defined
By the assumptions of others
Packaged and wrapped by certainties
I do not share. Forbidden to be myself
By absolutes that when unpicked are empty

It is taken for granted what is accepted
In a world of closely knitted cultural norms
Reinforced by ancient adage, enforced conformity
How can one breathe the freshness of
New ideas, see horizons to be explored
When all novelty is forbidden

There is another way, a different stroke
Interpretation free of prohibition
A long, slow gathering of hard won insight
That's not permitted by the righteous critic
No more informed than other tyrants of the centuries

This new truth has its own stamp
Protected under seal from trivialisation
It must be held with reverence, honoured
Not disdainfully poured out upon the earth
Pure, glistening water that gives us life

SIGNIFIER

The signature looked uniquely different in style
Although intended to be a facsimile of the others
A pattern repeated hundreds of times
Now appearing distinct in form, a new birthing

Is it that we never repeat ourselves precisely
Always being thrust into a novelty of expression
Recognised as still the true signifier
Yet a new appearing, a fresh appearing

As if remaining the same we constantly change
Seeking a fuller self expression in each act
Presenting to ourselves the samely different
Without permission seeking a further fullness

ONE

The crystal filled with pure water
Held up to the sun
Light indivisible through the whole
Fuses glass and liquid into one

So the life of spirit
Form and content co-inhere
Body and soul united, spun
Transfusing our sustentation fully begun

So easily missed, so easily overlooked
That which is unveiled presentness
Symbiotically bound to the other
The mystical, a noumenal togetherness
The broken-ness, the fragmentary, the separated
Are not the truth of seeing
Radiance is spread through the gift offered
Where we live and move and have our being

FALL

I am sorry
I didn't mean to fall
I have no memory of it
Only the cold, wet asphalt

Memory breaking into shards
Drifting away into nothingness
Without recognition
A life disappearing

I am sorry
I have done it this time
She will not come home
Again, the Doctor said

Walking along the long, bare
Hospital corridor alone
I felt encased in ice
I didn't mean to fall

She is taking home with her
Fading, as I am too

    Fadi...
        Fa...

ANOTHER PLACE

There is a darkness nearing
Imperceptible its appearing

Across neural synapses
A flow of gone away, of lapses

A silence creeping in cranial reaches
An inner sea of unknown breakers

Where muted bells and ocean swells
Rise to no new awakening. No spells

Wreak magic reversals
A time of repeated circles

Questions rarely answered
Memory unrewarded

What day is it today
Returns bright, unworn, fey

I name it from quicksand
And hold her hand

She in another place
And I, lost in soundless space

CAVE

They came out of the cave waters
The deadly tide, the sucking currents
The dark murky depths of death
Surging around them, grasping for them
The double image of life and lifelessness
Wrapped up in a womb of hope
Rushing into new life, a second birth
Born out of darkness into light
The baptism that is the invitation
To enter in, to be, to joyfully rejoice
Following the line that leads to celebration

SUFFERING

Why is suffering necessary
The pain that demands humility
The loss that sucks us empty
The dying that leaves nothing behind
The abandonment that breeds desolation

Here is the moment of anguish
The unrequited act, the final parting
I do not believe that everything has a reason
Much dumb, unredeemed happenstance
To be endured, to be despised, to be cast out

No happy endings, no coloured balloons
Only an eternal absence without warmth
A numbing of the heart, an iceberg overcoat
There is no seed, no flower, no celebration
Only fragments of a life lived, now gone

OTHER

There is a companionship
That has no easy naming
Embracing as an Autumn wind
Nourishing as Irish stew
Penetrating deep within
The fibres of the soul
A counterpoint to frailty
Succour in despair
Holding all stillness fecund
Bringing Advent promise
Covenantal presence
In encroaching darkness
To tell us once again
How to keep warm
Against the Winter chill
Reminding us always
Of otherness within
The shadow of a smile

CARERS ON NIGHT DUTY

The aged care staff wait her return
As usual the ambulance returns late
Pre-occupied with compounding duties
Multiplying beyond scheduled crises

In the small hours they blossom
Medical equipment readied, care in small packages
As matter as fact as celery, and as crisp
Determined to make pain redundant

Is it a matter of poise, or self acceptance
That leads them each night to acts of mercy
As normal as cheese crackers, brightness after dawn
With an easy competence wholly
Prepared for giving, as clouds for raining

A reflex born of holiness
Which is woven of warmth, presence, humility
The white paint on the refectory wall
Does not notice it reflects light in dark places

BEAUTY SALON

On entering we were embraced by the ambience
Of the oriental beauty salon
Incense fragrance drifting lightly
Water tumbling over black stones
In small ponds surrounded by bright green
Plants, source of exotic blooms
An air of mystic expectation

Dismissed to the waiting room
I wondered what arcane rites
Secret rituals, precious emulsions
Came into play as the magic
Of transformation took place
Within the distant murmur of voices
Overseeing the unfolding of ancient mysteries

My wife, radiant, appeared at the door
Clearly uplifted by the experience
'How was it?' I asked. 'Marvellous'
She replied. 'I did not understand a word'
The gaining of beauty it seems
Does not depend on communication
Only trust

DAY OF REST

Do you remember a time
When Sunday was a day of rest
A time for reflection, recovery
Quiet in which body idleness
And soul looked out across
Far distances in silence

Cricket was not played in the street
Loud parties suppressed, a sense of
Recessive reverence occupying inner
Canyons of the spirit where one
Felt noticed and attended to in an
Ambience of difference

To be cast aside and destroyed by
Lovers of capitalism who wanted
Bodies working without limits
To generate productivity
Dependent not upon inner gratitude
But outer possession of desired goods

The solemn remembrance of that quietude
Remains, giving to Sunday a vital specialness
Even now, when still, Church bells fill
The air with gratitude and praise while
Hard worked labourers rest tired bodies
Grateful for peace and solitude

You remember it don't you, that day
For stories, gentle laughter, and conversation
About the mystery of things and the magical
Drama of a creative Presence
Who, after labour, rested to recover, granting us
A time for meeting, belonging, celebrating

When following Church we gathered
To eat once a week a roast dinner
Amid the chatter of families and friends
Followed by reminiscences and gossip
On the shady verandah afterwards
Even a discussion of the sermon

Why such a precious gift was crudely
Thrust aside without thought I do not know
But surrounded now by loud, fretful sound
I hunger for the blessing of its restfulness
And the reassurance of life's human sharing
You do remember it, don't you

PAGEANTRY

I cannot enter into pageantry
That has a narrative
I do not share, no matter how compelling

There is a story embedded in its pomp
That is its justification
Weaving an unquestioned entitlement

There is no sense of marching on bones
Poisoned flesh decomposing to ensure Empire
A flag celebrating triumph without love

Yet in this matrix of display
There are those dignified and honourable
Paradoxically, seeking to be defenders of the faith

MEMORY LOSS

Like a child
I am being taught
Something necessary to do

My loved companion's illness
Unstoppable, flourishes
And I must serve

A commission of love
Returning love received
Unearned, taken for granted

The price to pay, patience
Learning humility
Fighting despair

Seeking meaning's acceptance
Giving a life in reply
For the life she willingly gave to me

SIMPLICITY

It is hard to be simple
With big ideas
Even the words droop
Struggling to breathe

Being simple is a gift
Aware of fundamentals
Disinterested in all else
What really matters known

I watch the moor hens
Wander across the road
Care for their young
Go home contented

Strange that the simple
Are truly wise
Uncomplicated, trusting
A wider kindness

I see him in church
Handicapped, happy
Living an inner peace
Source of grace to us all

NEXT

We will be carried smoothly in electric cars
Responsive to our spoken commands
Fed by machines, houses cleaned by robots
Homes heated and cooled by programmed need
Appliances and lights controlled by vocal instructions
Entertained in virtual environments of many forms
Soothed by drug regimes, plastic adaption, and enhancements
Dwellings fortified against unauthorised intrusion

Instructed, guided, reminded, assured, protected
Safe in our darkened cave staring at dancing shadows
Unmoved by risk, adventure, effort, achievement
Wondering at the slow dying of the light
Losing our life in the cocoon of pleasure's plenty
If we belong to the privileged and entitled, that is

Those not so blessed struggling for survival
Finding their life in scarcity and shared endeavour
Wind in their faces, rain on their fields
Facing daily hazard in nature's wide expanse
Companioned by joy, ambiguity, and forgiveness
In the testing of their humanness together
And the growth of their wings that lift them
Out of the cave into life

TRAJECTORY

What is God like, he said
Ten year old eyes wide

Consider the wind, I said
Wild, tumultuous, and noisy

Reshaping all that is
Rocks, landscapes, seas

Raucous, companionable, gentle
Guarantee of our every breath

Carrying life effortlessly
Into our deepest caverns

Against which we have no defence
Or need one

Spirit flow, lifting us as kites
Into the world's sky perspective

Holding us steady that we can see
Contours of the land we must cross

Guardian to guide us on our way
Blowing where it wills, where we are

Always moving on, calling
Making space for us to follow

END TIME

It is not my end
>That is troubling

But species extermination
>Leaving unanswered the question
>>What is it for

Illusion of smoke our cleverness
>Genius defeated by cosmic indifference

They gather to make quilts
>From bits and pieces creating glory

Perhaps it will be put together
>When it is over

SUNSET

IF TOMORROW NEVER COMES

If tomorrow never comes
Where will we be then
Unrealised in all our forms
The uselessness of when

All that we hope for gone
All that we are at end
No longer a life in stone
No messages to send

How long does now last
A moment, thick or thin
All that we are is past
No impulse to begin

This is the garment of time
We wrap around our heart
No river run, no summit climb
Of what are we a part

CONTEMPLATING

Is it duty that has suffocated us
No, more the modern spirit, relentlessly
Busy, indifferent, insensitive bogan-ness
That is contemptuous of non achievement
Addicted to performance, unacquainted with ambiguity

Taking away those inner riches gathered
From imitative speculation, mystical wanderings
Sweet slowness of reading, reflecting, meditating
The days of bush fragrance in dappled sunlight
Passing granite boulders on narrow tracks, in step

In a phrase, contemplation of existence
In it mysterious binding and unfairness
The fateful stroke of time's pendulum
Far distant cry of wild geese calling to us
Telling us, do not forget to wonder

But the modern spirit strips away the green
The gentle incense drift, the candle flicker
Those subtle triggers of a surer spirit
Waiting, purposing stillness, learning to trust
Contemplating being here a simple gladness

UNKNOWING

Unknowing is a wandering path
Let the world speak
Stay open to direction

Here is the making of the self
Within defencelessness
Key to an inner dwelling

Inarticulate is the pointing word
That leads to listening space
Hearing both blood and bone

Feeling the language of longing
Yearning for life's touch
In boundless open-ness

So easy to be still
To rest apace
To earth peace

AS IS

Those things that matter, simple and true
Obvious in their complicity are
Common as the morning dew

As natural as the normal
Pristine, as always new
Reassuring as the usual

Found in the daily order
Testimony in the patterned round
Assuring a present augur

Where from the small and hidden
The pulse of purpose found
Growth rises as if bidden

Sight to the looking eye
Light to the travelling feet
Bedrock of the spinning gyre

ONLY A WIND

The other side of early light
Has no direction where to move
Transition signalled but not defined
Only a wind of persistent pushing

The snake, sacred in its tattooed swiftness
Sheds its skin when transition comes
Leaving behind its once upon a time, discerning
Only a wind of persistent pushing

Here is the dawn of a new beginning
Cosmic-shaped, riddled with destiny's veins
Rhythmic beat upon the prelude's naming
A wind of persistent pushing

ENIGMA

I am a poem
Read differently
By curious readers

The text translated
Into many languages
With varying success

In the mirror
The image simmers
With inconstancy

A self un-manifest
Child of many glances
Little understood

Yet the poem
States its truth
I do not yet grasp

GRAMMAR

In the birthing of wonder, that unexpected surprising
Moment that comes unannounced, there is a constant
Not associated with nature's splendour or the
Astonishing creativity within human inventiveness
But that out of the blind silence of nothingness
When all resources seem to have failed
Thought, vision, speech emerge, as Pascal claimed

There comes into being a burgeoning significance
That takes your breath away, confirming that
When we look into the abyss, out comes
A presentiment of possibility, confronting us
With the truth that in the depth there
Is more than we can imagine or know
Beyond our capacity to articulate its spawning wealth

A new language that only love can interpret
Whose grammar has to be learned slowly, with an other

OLD FRIENDS

Old friends take a lifetime to mature
They do not spring early from conjoint activity
But grow slowly into mountain gums

As trustworthy as coin of the realm
To be spent in need, kept for rainy days
Treasured beyond all desiring

They understand without speech
Give without explanation
Act instinctively to deflect harm

Without question, beyond reward
As naturally to be cherished
As the perfume of a rose

Oasis in the desert
Refuge in the storm
Fire-light in snow drift

Here bread broken
Wine shared
Life made companionable

PICK AND SHOVEL DESTINY

The archaeologist and her team
Discovered a buried city
Below centuries of over-burden
Judged to be of 400 B. C. identity

A lively placed filled with those
Confident of eternity's reassurance
Assured of a valuable place in time
Permanently established significance

But time is a fickle companion
Setting free forces of uncaring change
The city lived and died as all created things
And disappeared from sight and history's page

So it will be with our besieged generations
The earth, still incomplete, will redesign
All of the greatness we applauded
Will disappear under rubble and dusty grime

Will there be shining values to be claimed by others
Who scrape with spade and fork to quantify
Shards of a civilisation lost to itself forever
What will they treasure? What decry

MUSIC

The only proof he needed
For the existence of God
    Was music

                Kurt Vonnegut. *Epitaph*

We enter into a festive environment
Offering tonal pathways fantastical
Leading into mystical dimensions
Receivers of exotic madrigals

Flooding us with cascading richness
Ephemeral, encompassing surround
Exploding sensitivities, rationalities
Elusiveness beyond profound

Life for the failing spirit
Tonic for the gasping soul
Effervescence of a bell's eternal chime
Advancing, fading, transmogrifying foil

Entering in, vibrating resonance
In every fibre, every ear
Carrying harmonics of the heart
Radiance of the now, the then, the here

SHIPWRECKED

Now retired, sitting around cafe tables
Not accepting their invisibility, a disappeared generation
Suffering with no flock to shepherd, cast aside
Without a secure harbour where they are celebrated

The ship they called the Church beached
On dry land, its remnant sailors now on perilous seas
Where the anchor weight of systematised theology
Cannot hold against raging currents

Carried in small, unstable craft, they look hopefully for
A figure walking in the storm's heart, speaking peace
But the word they seek is silent, eaten by the acids of contradiction
A generation travelling without compass into a gathering tempest

How could they have missed the weather turn
The message that time had moved beyond
A conceit that God's wind had been captured dogmatically
Which is to say domesticated, and brought submissively to heel

The horizons they canvass are blurred
Landlocked, they are out of touch with tides
Reshaping the landscapes, the given undermined by rips
Carrying away the debris of centuries

They gather in the shadow of depleted thought
Protecting a cargo that has lost its value
Since, too long unturned, it has rotted through
Its ancient ritual and unrequited gestures

They faithfully repeat remembered lore
Re-hearse the dictums, re-examine the charts
The small vessels have sailed long since
They are not on them

BIRTHDAY PARTY

The birthday party celebrated
One hundred and forty years
Outcome of Covid separation
This gathering combined 50 years
For their daughter, 90 for her mother
A time of delighted festival at last

Old age itself has no necessary weight
Whether young or old, the count of years
Guarantee nothing at all, except survival
But here, the evident love and joy between
Mother and daughter gave time its meaning

DICTATOR

Can one find home again
If the people are betrayed
Can one stand un-judged
If the truth has been suppressed
Is there a way to redemption
If no repentance is entertained
Can one stay cleanly alive
After condemning others to death
Can one be unafraid
If hollow deep within
Is there a road to follow
When the Devil claims his debt
The hammer and the sickle
Have no honour to confer

Only the abyss. Only the abyss
Death's final greeting. Death's final kiss

WHISTLE BLOWER

The new standard lamp
An arc of L.E.D. thinness
Reaches to bend over
As if crushed by duty

The light spills warmly around
But looking closely, like sorrowful rain
Ribbons of phosphorescence fall down
The long, stretched length

Giving an impression of pain
Even suffering, as if exploited
Offering all it can, at awful cost
With no escape, no reward

It is the irony of social deceit
That those who shed light
Are punished for their integrity
Another whistle blower sent to jail

BRAWL

There drifted over us
A sense of isolation, a sense of detachment
Watching the fight of drunken teenagers
In the grassed hollow by the railway station

Light glinting on knives, disassociated awareness
Of outcomes and looming penalties
As if the sacrifice of the future
Meant nothing to blood lust rage

And we, powerless to intervene
Reason and considered judgment
Was not the coinage of exchange
Was it fear, malice, self hatred

That generated the meaningless encounter
Where life-death consequences
Seemed of little matter in a hostile exchange
Oblivious that the blood shed was that of brothers

PAYING ATTENTION

The boat, fashioned by our experience
Drifted imperceptibly away, unnoticed in the gloom
The fleet gathered for its own purposes
Setting its own course, hoisting its own sails

We in the darkness felt the sea brooding
Time had taught us when the weather changed
The air carried its rising intention
Water began to lap at our craft's side

We watched the fleet glide away
The sounds of song and clinking glasses carried
Telling of an unawareness of a coming tempest
Deep currents turning, the sea wrack rehearsing

We could have told them to attend
To prepare, batten down, to reef the sails
But it would have been wasted effort
For they had not yet met Leviathan

Each generation in its turn, brought to reality
We sail upon the surface only, most of the time
It is in the vortex of the deep our lives are won
Or lost, determined by the discipline of paying attention

GROWLING GRASS FROG ENIGMA

The sentinel sent off his warning
As I took my first step on the path
Girding the edge of the wetland ponds
Growling grass frog signalling my aim to pass

Each step along eliciting an aware note
Following my trajectory with stated intent
The chorus my accompanying sound
As if their company chanted consent

Was it a warning, telling of a deadly event
Or, paradoxically, an invitation that bespoke
I walked within a cloud of ambiguity
Could it be they wanted me to croak

SUDDENLY

His voice was flat
All vitality fled
He held his mobile
Not knowing
What it was
A slip of the finger
Called a family member
His legendary eloquence
Reduced to monosyllables
Incomprehensibility reigned
Turning, direction dissolved
Space without affect, form
He was once again
A small boy
Lost in confusion

ATTENTION

Shared experience over many years
Is a richness beyond price
Telling of a common way
Where life was renewed
Again and again
Within the embrace of intimacy
Child of struggle, effort, hope
In trust of the other
Who understood without words
The mutual need to be esteemed

TIME PASSING

Grief is the price we pay for love
Kingfisher splash in the blue pond water
Butterfly flutter on bright green ponds
Out in the sunlight your joyous laughter

Memory holds such a small part of wonder
The stumbling misunderstanding, unfailing nurture
See how the owl drifts silently yonder
The ants run in lines to verdant pastures

I remember the small things, the alive gestures
Eyes closed in delight, the sharp buzz of flies
All in the complex, bees fuss over the hive
The hurt of rejection, half truths, half lies

Now in the twilight of clocks and night chorus
What comes forward is a desire to cherish
The moments when life paused to take a deep breath
When we looked at each other without blemish

SANCTUARY

Where can we find sanctuary
In this time-space world
That has lost confidence in itself

Where can we find refuge
For we have been stolen away
Abandoned in a dark wood

Those impulses that heal and complete
The things in us we treasure
Are dispersed, directions and purposes undermined

A shadowing without consciousness
Without words, without memory, without air
Unacquainted with gentleness, enchanted lingering

Once being-here was setting the fire after school
Preparing the stove to cook the evening meal
A warm kitchen, busy chatter, loving enfoldment

So simple the act of being home, secure
Gone now in fear's uncertainty of tomorrow
Searching for sanctuary, refuge, and trust

TRIAL

The way to school was a mythical journey, not understood
First, the wide creek to cross, speaking of baptism's second birth
The river's golden glitter gone, these many years past
The trial by water

Beyond the vast dark garden-park, stretching away
Within which nature reigned fertile, fickle, fey
Yellow, orange leaves, wet upon the strand, a threat
The trial of earth

Rising to the path between primary, secondary schools
Arenas of struggle, test, and challenge
Within the quadrangle, humiliation and command
The trial of fire

Still higher, the path mounts into the realms of play
Athletics, tennis, swimming, the City oval
Each stadium a new beginning of the fight
The trial of courage

Still higher yet, the pinnacle
A poppet head, three storeys high
The last ascent, the last enhancement
The trial of hope

Upon the top level of the tower
Direction named, distance spelled out

Overlooking the world in all its aspects
The trial of humility

Back down the steps to the City of gold
Past play, knowledge, growth, and limitation
Onto the chosen way, an open destiny
The trial of freedom

DREAM

The dream was a grey landscape of war
Denuded ash undergrowth, stick figure trees
Soldiers in serge suits and battle dress
In learned conversation of what frees

Tall, erudite singleness, resigned to lack of colour
One by one falling in a final expiring
Without vitality, purpose, or planned endeavour
Dispirited, unmotivated, dying

A battle field blanket flung over our future
Futility and rectitude aligned in shadow
The technicolour exuberance of nature
Expunged from the malefic, wretched hallows

Whence this despairing sorrow
Unconscious prophesy of the troubled deep
Backward glance at past harrows
Prescience of a nuclear Winter we shall meet

JAZZ PIANO

Pure, simple sounds
From the jazz piano
It is that simplicity
And fidelity we seek

Not a life crowded
With unrepeatable offers
Of those things
I do not need

A life harassed by accumulations
Pressured by importunity
Detailing what I must have
To be whole

No, it is the flawless gift
A cadence of crystal sound
That tells me again
Of human warmth enfolded

DAFFODIL SEASON

It is daffodil season, so much unsayable
So little comes to voice from the
Address of daffodil clusters fully bloomed
Along the Village paths, beyond the wetlands

Not that there is wanting material for response
So much of life is elusive, inchoate
Beyond the reach of words, of language's grasp
Why then to write more than 'daffodil season'

Calling up a sense of yellow fragility
Of some inner felicity of grace
Carrying a gentle image to sensibility
Standing up with pride of beauty's face

One sees with joy this sentinel of Spring
The coming of that golden poem
Which cannot be expressed in any fulsome way
Evading all attempts, except to say, 'Spring has come'

Here painful limitation before nature's splendour
Surrounded by fragrance we cannot touch
Bursting forth, spreading, enveloped in beauty's realm
A realm no word can breach, or yet approach

MARY

Asked to draw a symbol
Of her life she drew a candle
Reflective of her wholeness
Clear as the wick's light
Devoted, uncomplicated, clever
A nun who lived as tallow of the holy

I knew her, said Jessup, in the conflict
When tribes fought tribes for illusive honour
She kept the school open, her flock close
Protecting them by force of personality
Dedicated commitment, an iron will
It did not save her. She perished with them

Every time I light a candle
I think of Mary. To bring light
She burned her life away in love
The way by which her pupils walked
Jessup poked the fire, sparks shooting up
All Saints day tomorrow. Darkness does not prevail

DOLL'S HOUSE

Capitalism is a doll's house
Immaculately conceived
Conceptually trivial, cruelly indifferent
Filled with the illusion of delight
Promising securities as phantom
As bit-coin money piles

Here is the surprise. When you seek
To enter you discover doors and windows
Are only painted on. It offers only outside
Inside one guesses empty rooms and halls
If one found a magic key to enter in
Only loss and disappointment calls

Engaging in a process of emptying us out
Unconcerned with inwardness shrinking
Within our entertained self, becoming
Hollow, becoming rootless, becoming imitative
Of a way of being human, truly infantile
Plastic in fabric and in essence too

The house is small. But convenient with
A sharp eye for advantage. If you look hard
Enough you will see fairy floss for sale
That deadly sugar that sweetly plots demise
Of space and time, but not desire

Is there light within, a stillness necessary for beauty
Something offering a kinship for the soul
Uncontaminated by the smell of decay
A body of ideas not looted for their profit
A recognition of enough. An un-compromised divine
That has no price tag fixing its claim

There seems to be no interplay between
Inwardness and outwardness
No seeing underneath, no presence to remind
That we connect with truth and harmony sublime
Can I find here other than the counterfeit enshrined
Inside there are only dolls

REMEMBRANCE

A long, brown extension table
Large candlestick holders, soldier straight
Define the laid out order of the feast

It is remembrance day again
Around the napkin splendour
Fourteen war widows gather once more

They are old now. Their vitality survived the trenches
Greetings, laughter, eating, drinking, chattering
Sorrow has long since fled. But is not dead

SLAUGHTER

Dust encased cattle mobs
Desecrated our street cricket wicket
On the way to the sale yards
Tom was fatalistic each time

His father, who worked at the abattoirs
Invited us to his work place
Where young men with sledge hammers
Waited for terrified, squealing pigs

In the evenings, bare feet and bottled beer
He sang Galway Bay, fixing me with
An accusing eye for my complicity
In Irish misery and suffering

I grew up feeling half responsible for the
Irish troubles. Was it something I said.
I don't remember. But not the slaughter
Of doomed pigs. That I remember

CATHEDRAL

Behind the ancient stone Cathedral
Beneath the generous branched guardian tree
Warm in the sun
She approached me, engaging, committed

Wearing her Smith Family credentials proudly
She talked of how one in seven children
Are afflicted by poverty
A circumstance she sought to overcome

Across the square another young woman
With tattooed arm lifted to her lips
An e-cigarette to express clouds
Of smoke into the innocent air

One giving her life away
One blowing her life away
Both warm in the sun
Behind a stone Cathedral

Ent
—

The great Oak commands its hospitality
Be honoured, stretching wide, welcoming
Casting shade upon the rain blessed earth
A place of retreat to all comers seeking nutrient soil

We gather beneath its beneficence gratefully
Protected from brisk winds, indifferent traffic
The sharp blade of technological destruction
In leaf nurture, cosmic nobility, sombre integrity

This abiding, this relational event, a spirit-indwelling
Carrying narratives beyond a hundred years
Telling us its deepest secret, the seed is still within
Nothing over time has diminished the desire to give praise

The acorn is more than nature in its symbolic cachet
Holding intact a monument of presence, of mothering
Demonstrating the beauty of the solitary self
In its foundational truth of wanting companionship

We sit without agenda or necessity, enfolded
Whispers from rustling leaves, creaking from living limbs
Whose task is reassurance, whose mission is stability
That we might learn in this turning world, trust in foreverness

And you, in your quiet sojourn, wondering
What question will I ask

STORIES

Now that God is in exile
What does she do all day
Apart from gather and prepare food
Collect water from the stream
Wash clothes with other travellers

All of that. But mostly she tells stories
To the children after their baths
To wives sharing lunch
To tired workmen, when delivering
Morning and afternoon tea

So it is they go their way
Discussing what was meant
By the tales they heard
Being fed by their possibility
Sustained by their hidden purpose

Sometimes they lament their exile
Its privations, its suffering, its wounds
Growing to understand however that
Without the daily struggle of their estate
They would never have heard the stories of life

www.ingramcontent.com/pod-product-compliance
Lightning Source LLC
Chambersburg PA
CBHW012005090526
44590CB00026B/3881